Sand Surprise

by Jack Lewis
illustrated by Luke Jurevicius and Toby Quarmby

Copyright © by Harcourt, Inc.

All rights reserved. No part of this publication may be reproduced or transmitted in any form or by any means, electronic or mechanical, including photocopy, recording, or any information storage and retrieval system, without permission in writing from the publisher.

Requests for permission to make copies of any part of the work should be addressed to School Permissions and Copyrights, Harcourt, Inc., 6277 Sea Harbor Drive, Orlando, Florida 32887-6777. Fax: 407-345-2418.

HARCOURT and the Harcourt Logo are trademarks of Harcourt, Inc., registered in the United States of America and/or other jurisdictions.

Printed in the United States of America

ISBN 10: 0-15-350621-0
ISBN 13: 978-0-15-350621-5

Ordering Options
ISBN 10: 0-15-350598-2 (Grade 1 On-Level Collection)
ISBN 13: 978-0-15-350598-0 (Grade 1 On-Level Collection)
ISBN 10: 0-15-357777-0 (package of 5)
ISBN 13: 978-0-15-357777-2 (package of 5)

If you have received these materials as examination copies free of charge, Harcourt School Publishers retains title to the materials and they may not be resold. Resale of examination copies is strictly prohibited and is illegal.

Possession of this publication in print format does not entitle users to convert this publication, or any portion of it, into electronic format.

1 2 3 4 5 6 7 8 9 10 179 15 14 13 12 11 10 09 08 07 06

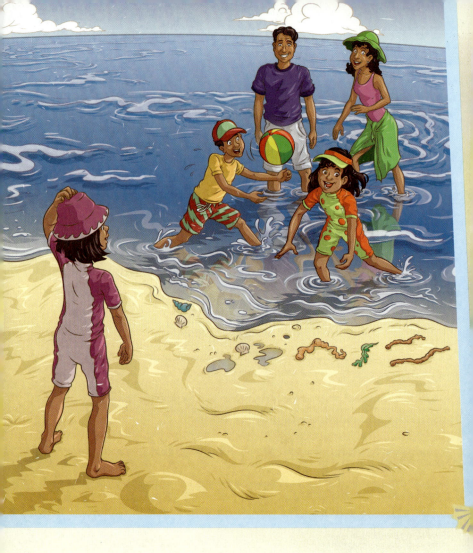

Our family went to the shore for the day. We went swimming in the water.

We started digging in the sand. We made a mouse. There were some sticks on the sand. We put them on the mouse.

The three of us put shells all over the sand mouse. It looked pretty. We made a moat by the sand mouse.

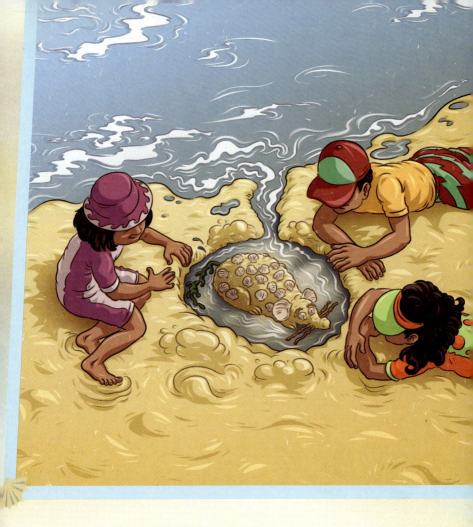

The water came up and filled the moat. The sand mouse looked as if it were swimming.

Some people came over to us. "It will be a surprise when we show them our sand mouse," I said.

"We like your sand toad," they said.

The water had come all the way up over the sand mouse! Some of the sand and sticks had come off.

It *was* a toad!

"What a surprise," I said. "Our mouse has turned into a toad!"

Think Critically

1. What did the children make?

2. How did the mouse change during the story?

3. How do you think the children felt when they saw what happened to the mouse?

4. Who is telling this story? How do you know?

5. Did the children make a good choice when they made a moat around the mouse? Why or why not?

 Social Studies

Write Sentences The children worked together to make their sand mouse. Write three sentences about things you should remember when working together with other people.

 **School-Home Connection** Read *Sand Surprise* to a family member. Talk about different things that you can make with sand.

Word Count: 143